FUSED

FUSED

poems by
Gloria Heffernan

SHANTI ARTS PUBLISHING

BRUNSWICK, MAINE

FUSED

Published by Shanti Arts Publishing

Designed by Shanti Arts Designs

Cover image—*Perfect Green* by Wendy
Harris; used with her permission

Shanti Arts LLC
193 Hillside Road
Brunswick, Maine 04011
shantiarts.com

Printed in the United States of America

ISBN: 978-1-962082-65-5 (softcover)

LCCN: 2025935061

For Jim
My husband, best friend, first reader
and
Anam Cara

Contents

Acknowledgments

The author wishes to thank the editors of these journals in which the following poems were first published:

Animal Grace, chapbook published by Seven Kitchens Press: "The Earth Moved" and "What a person wants"

Autumn Sky Poetry DAILY: "Animal Grace"

Blue Heron Review: "Encounter on Route 169"

The Chestnut Review: "Reflexology Lesson"

Drunk Monkeys: "Algorithm and Blues"

Griffel: "Mr. Gutenberg Respectfully Declines Mr. Zuckerberg's Friend Request"

Gyroscope Review Online: "Elegy for the Magi Trees"

Hail to the Symptom, chapbook published by Moonstone Press: "Flight", "Life Lines", and "Prayer for a Miracle in the Newsroom"

The Healing Muse: "Call Button", "E. R. Takayama, Japan", "Fused", "Legacy", "The Nurse Who Brushed Your Hair", "Out-Patient Surgery", and "What the Map Makers Knew"

Hole in the Head Review: "Murmuration" and "Meeting Emily"

Intima: "Proxy"

Iris Literary Journal: "Mud Season"

Last Stanza Journal: "Five Things to Never Write a Poem About"

Miracle Monocle: "What is More Generous than a Window?"

Mizmor Anthology, Poetica Publishing Company: "You Just Never Know"

Naugatuck River Review: "At the Blind Poet's Reading, I Contemplate Deafness" (winner of the 2022 *Naugatuck River Review* Narrative Poetry Prize)

New York Quarterly: "Love Letter to a Stranger"

Nine Mile Journal: "Adirondack Morning Meditation"

One Art: "It Figures" and "Instructions for the Morning after the Terrible Haircut"

Origami Poems Project: "Gratitude"

The Perch, Yale School of Medicine: "Cardio-in-Place"

Peregrine: "Visitation"

Plainsongs: "Four Seasons" and "The Harlot's Version"

Poems, for Now, supplement to *River Heron Review:* "Epistle to Jack Gilbert after Rereading 'A Brief for the Defense'"

Pure Slush: "Planning the Funeral"

Quarter(ly): "Assembling the Perfect Father" and "Rise"

Silver Birch Press: "Epithalamion for Margie and Ed"

Sisyphus: "Fault Lines"

Stone Canoe: "An Invisible Form of Sadness" and "Nice Boys"

Third Wednesday: "Vigil" and "What to Say When"

Word Peace: "Mother's Day"

A Word of Thanks for the Cover Art

One of the first lessons we learn when we begin our lives as readers is, *Don't judge a book by its cover.* But I want to challenge that dearly held adage.

I would be honored to have this book judged worthy of the painting that appears on its cover. It was painted by my dear friend, Wendy Harris, an award-winning artist who generously permitted me to use *Perfect Green* for the cover of this collection.

This painting, like all of Wendy's work, celebrates the beauty of nature, the play of light and shadow, and the interconnectedness of all living things. It reminds us that, like the trees she has so lovingly rendered on canvas, we are dependent on each other for shelter, for shade, and for the very air we breathe. Such is the spirit of *Fused*.

Gloria Heffernan

Fused

I could not hear the blood
entering my vein
one drop at a time all night long.

Four pints. Four donors.
Four faces I would never see.
Hands I would never touch.

I could not hear their voices—
the languages they spoke,
the prayers they prayed.

I did not know what car they drove,
or who they voted for or why.
But I knew I would die without them.

I knew the rupture in my body
would only be healed
because four strangers said yes.

And now, I cannot look
at the woman in the grocery store,
or the man who cut me off in traffic,

or the people in line at the voting booth,
without wondering,
Did you save my life?

The Hope Machine

—after Ada Limón's "The Quiet Machine"

I'm learning so many different ways to be hopeful. To ignore all the logical reasons that tell me to accept despair as a given. To wake up in the morning and still brush my teeth and wash my face and sprinkle my coffee with cinnamon. I am learning to hope because the children I love need to see me sitting beside them in the boat, oar in hand, rowing with them on the river that carries us all. I am learning to hope that hope is not a feeling but a decision, and one I can make every day, just as naturally as I decide to wear a coat when it is cold out or eat soup when I need nourishment. I am learning that hope is food and water and air and breath. I am learning that hope is not the thing with feathers but rather the thing with sturdy shoes that walks out into the elements and keeps moving over the broken sidewalks and the mud puddles and the snowbanks and the fields of grass, and whatever terrain comes along. That is how this machine works.

Epistle to Jack Gilbert after Rereading "A Brief for the Defense"

Dear Jack,
I have been rowing for days and the music
feels as far away as the shore.
Is there still laughter in the streets of Calcutta?
It's so hard to hear over the coughing
and the gasping for breath.
I admit there will be music despite everything,
even if I can't hear it.
But how can I live in the midst of it all
and still dare to risk delight?
That miraculously fashioned Bengal tiger
you describe so vividly is nearing extinction.
And so, I fear, are we.
But you tell me to be stubbornly grateful—
even as the furnace is stoked by hatred and greed
and its ravenous flames heat the planet day by day.
I believed you when you told me to enjoy my life
because that's what God wants.
I bathed in those words like cool water.
I refused to praise the Devil.
I want to believe you Jack, but the flies.
Their incessant buzzing.
They are more stubborn than my gladness.
I will keep on rowing,
but oh, my arms are tired.

Animal Grace

I have tried all the prayers my mother taught me
kneeling by the bedside when I was five.
They're all good, but they've never felt like me.

I have tried Namaste and Shalom and Amen
because I know words matter and I want to choose
wisely from the lexicon of peace.

But it wasn't until I saw the three-legged pit-bull
bounding across the playground
that a prayer rose to my lips that finally said,

Yes, this is my psalm.
This is the hymn I will carry in my heart
until the day I die.

And so, I begin the day with these words.
Dear Lord, let me greet every person
who crosses my path as if they were a dog.

Let my face light up with joy and curiosity.
Let my hand reach out with tenderness and care.
Let me see and celebrate their eagerness to love.

Let me offer up bowls of food and soft blankets.
Let me pause and gaze into their deep warm eyes.
Let me trust their capacity for goodness.

When I find a person who has been mistreated,
who growls like a hungry cur in a dark alley,
let me approach cautiously, but approach, nonetheless.

When I see one who is hungry
and trembling in a doorway, let me share
with them whatever is mine to give.

Let me love first and ask questions later.
Let me see in their eyes the answer
to the only question that matters.

No matter the pedigree, no matter the mix,
Let me see a creature whose only job
is to be loved.

Moments of Color and Cloud

—for Wendy Harris

She is closing her studio,
removing the paintings from the walls,
adjusting to the reality of Alzheimer's disease,
a moniker she wears now
the way she has worn Artist for forty years.

Her canvases shimmer with light and shadow,
the dew-drenched radiance
of an Adirondack lake at dawn,
a two-lane highway unfurling
between fields of new-mown hay,
a pillar of sun piercing the blue
and crimson clouds of twilight.

She is a curator of moments.
Moments of blessing, moments of pain.
Moments that beg to be recalled,
and moments that, once lost,
will never be missed.

These are not paintings.
These are moments of color and cloud.
These are the ineffable
rendered into the timeless.

Do not paint her in shades of decline.
Lost keys, irretrievable passwords,
a pot left too long on the stove,
a face untethered from a name.
An inventory of evidence
that verifies the diagnosis.
But a diagnosis is not an identity.

She is not a portrait of decline.
She is a landscape in transition
picking up a new brush,
capturing a new moment,
and another, and another.

She is an alchemist who has spent her life
transforming paint into gold.
Now she faces a new canvas on which
she will transform loss into discovery.

Elegy for the Magi Trees

I called them the Magi Trees
since the first time I saw them.
Three giant Norway Spruce
just behind the rise of the drumlin
beyond our backyard.

Regal trees bearing wisdom and gifts,
always on the verge of scaling that small hill,
always on the brink of arrival.

For years, I watched them reveal
themselves in the dimmest early morning light,
drinking my coffee before sunrise
under their watchful presence.

In winter darkness,
when frost tipped their branches,
they shimmered in the moonlight
as if all the constellations
had descended for just a few hours
to rest on their limbs,
and offer a night light to the deer
reclining in the bend of their roots.

And then the heavy equipment.
The roar of the chain saws.
The descent, one after the other,
like innocent men lined up
before a firing squad.
I watched, gutted, nothing to do but witness.
Woodchippers made quick work
of the remains.
Later in the day, I walked to the site,
gathered three pinecones.
Carried them home.

The World Is Tired

The world is tired,
as I am tired,
as you are tired.

Parents, tired as they try
to keep their children
safe and happy, and
learning, and living.

Nurses, tired as they try
to have hope even when called
to be the last hand held,
the last voice heard.

The world is tired,
is hobbling, is hoping.
The world is calling
for compassion, for patience.

I adopt a new mantra.
Everyone is trying their best . . .
I try to remember to repeat it over
and over again—

in the supermarket,
in the doctor's waiting room,
at the kitchen table
looking out at the bird feeders
that need to be filled again.

The world is tired. So tired.
So broken. So precious.
So desperate for rest
as we go on trying day after day,
trying to do the best we can.

For My 63rd Birthday I Receive My First Set of Hearing Aids

Today, I am being fitted with my new
high-tech hearing aids—compact, Blue-Tooth ready,
matched to my skin-tone to blend discretely
behind my ear even if I put my hair up in a ponytail.
They've thought of everything.
Except for what I will be better equipped to hear:

> Another war to end all wars pummels Ukraine.
> The climate surges as the UN declares a planetary crisis.
> Polar bears top the endangered species list.
> Sky-rocketing gas prices warn us not to go too far.

The audiologist adjusts the volume,
treble, bass to customize the sound.
My voice echoes like Lucy Ricardo
with her head stuck in a trophy.
My hair rattles against my collar
like the crumpling of parchment.
My fingers on the keyboard
tap like Shirley Temple
dancing on the silver-screen.
The sounds are strangely familiar
but out of proportion.
The doctor tells me I will adjust,
that my brain will get used to it.

> In the meantime, the world cries out.
> In the meantime, thousands huddle
> in a subway station in Kyiv—no food, no toilets.
> In the meantime, the groaning of the planet
> grows louder and more persistent.
> And even if I remove the devices,
> I cannot turn a deaf ear to the suffering.

Flight

First international flight.
My best friend pokes my arm
and shakes her head looking
at my disembarkation card.
You're an American, she says,
pointing to Line 5: Nationality.
I have answered Irish—
just as I do whenever anyone asks.
You're only Irish in America, she says,
as the jet roars across the Atlantic
to the nation of my grandparents.
*Better take another look
at your passport*, she laughs.
I erase the line and change my answer.
Line 5: American. A simple fix.

Four decades later,
four passports expired and renewed,
I am still an American,
even as my country struggles
to remember what that means.
I learned I was American
when I traveled far from home.
Now those who travel here
to become Americans
are told to go back
to their shit-hole countries.
What will they need to erase?
Into what land
will they disembark?

Vigil

I know how it feels
to sit at the bedside
in a hospice room,
watching.

I know the smells
that permeate the air
surrounding a loved one
whose time is running out—
bleached sheets and a faint odor
of unwashed hair.

I know the halting rise
and fall of the chest,
have listened to the labored breathing
not knowing whether to pray
for the next breath or the final one.

I know the precise yet tender gestures
of caregivers doing what they can
to keep the patient comfortable,
without hope of healing,
seeking only a peaceful transition.

Twenty years ago,
it was my mother.
Today it is my planet.

Life Lines

—after Wendell Berry's "The Peace of Wild Things"

When despair grows in me,
and I cannot read another headline
telling me that
hatred holds the winning hand,
I go to my desk where paper and pen wait.
I think of those I love and write
the words that pierce the dark.
Thank you. I love you. I wish you peace.
Love letters to the people
whose very existence cools
the fever of hopelessness. And for a time,
I rest in the grace of gratitude and am free.

Mother's Day

Dear Mother,
Do you remember when
I was a child and we sang
"He's Got the Whole World in His Hands"
every Sunday at the folk mass?
I imagined your face cradled
in God's strong, warm palms.
Were they too warm, Mother?
Is that why your glaciers are melting?
Did those hands squeeze too tight?
Is that why the volcanoes are erupting?
I'm worried about you, Mother.
I'm afraid you may have fallen
into the wrong hands.

Dear Child,
The only hands I am in are yours,
and all your sisters and brothers.
Hands that clear-cut my forests,
and forge islands out of plastic.
Hands that wring oil from my veins,
and dump chemicals into my oceans.
Don't worry about God's hands, my child.
Worry about your own.
Worry when they reap the harvest
of convenience and waste,
worry about how you will wash
the stain of complicity
from under your own fingernails.

Pompeii

I keep wanting to talk about it
in the past tense,
as if it were a distant memory,
a season that came and went,
arrayed in its own distinct
yet temporary color:
> *Spring green*
> *Autumn gold*
> *Summer blue*
> *Winter white*
But what color does a pandemic wear?

Six seasons and counting,
shrouded in grey
like ash settling over the year,
the detritus of a volcano
that never ceases emptying itself
onto everything in its path.

Centuries hence,
we will be excavated by archeologists
who will analyze how it all unfolded.
They will study shards of plastic
that once held Purell,
pantries stockpiled with toilet paper,
journals laden with grief and fear.

Wearing gloves and masks,
they will take notes, label artifacts,
reverently brush away
the dust that fills every crevice.

They will pinpoint the moment
when the eruption began,
stopping us all mid-breath.
They will sell tickets, guide tours,
tell the story to anyone
left to listen.

Cardio-in-Place

One month into the Covid lockdown,
we look out the window at a scrim of April snow
after five days of unrelenting rain.
Donning bathrobes and slippers,
we grab hand-weights dusty from disuse, and try a new strategy:
marching from room to room
making up lyrics to John Philip Sousa's greatest hits.

Pumping our arms, we stomp from our bedroom to the guest room
where tumbleweeds of dog hair pool under the dresser.
Then down the hall to the living room
where last week's newspapers are stacked on the floor
next to a month's worth of *New Yorkers* which we have actually read
instead of merely skimming the cartoons and puzzling over the poems.

Lifting our knees higher, we swing the dumbbells in unison
as we stride through the kitchen, past the refrigerator
and the pantry I have organized alphabetically by soup and bean variety,
then downstairs to the basement, around the woodshop,
past the washer-dryer, and the spare futon
where the grandkids congregate during holiday sleepovers.
Marching back up the stairs to repeat the circuit,
we urge each other on for the next lap as Max falls in behind us,
tail wagging though clearly confused by the sudden flurry of activity.

I wonder what the neighbors would think if they walked past the window
and caught a glimpse of us in our pajamas parading from room to room.
But I don't worry about it since they are too busy draping sheets
over their kitchen tables to build forts for desperately bored children
who cannot bear to watch another episode of *Umizoomi*,
or play one more round of *I Spy* on Zoom with tech-weary grandparents.

Four laps later, we have traded Sousa for Springsteen,
and even if we weren't "Born to Run," we keep going,
certain the endorphins will kick in any minute now.
Stopping to catch our breath, we look out the picture window
where the magnolia tree blooms under a light veil of snow.

We are safe at home where our greatest burden is the privilege
of boredom.
Our lungs are full and functioning. We are together.
I can't complain.

Out-Patient Surgery

I have made the bed
and washed the breakfast dishes.
My dishes.
Because you have been fasting since midnight.
Standard pre-surgical procedures.
In and out by noon, they tell us.
Nothing to worry about.

But I do worry,
because I am not there where I should be,
sitting in a hard plastic chair
drinking coffee that has cooled to lukewarm
while I wait for someone in scrubs
to come out and tell me
you are fine.

Instead of holding your hand
as they wheel you into the OR,
I squeeze it once and let go
as a masked nurse escorts you
from the car to the lobby
before I drive off to wait
for the phone to ring.

Necessary precautions, they tell us.
This is how we flatten the curve.
They call it out-patient surgery.
But I am the one who is out,
and anything but patient
as I wait here at home
for news of you.

Tranquility Recollected

I breathe deeply recalling the empty beach
at Montauk Point more than a decade ago
in that muted moment before sunrise
when the sky unfolds from midnight blue to mauve.
Inhale . . . Exhale . . . Slowly . . . Each breath
keeping pace with the waves lapping the shoreline,
bare feet planted in cool sand,
arms extended in the Peaceful Warrior pose.

I had forgotten the quiet rhythm of conscious breathing,
the sense of peace that carried me on its waves
while my lungs filled and emptied, filled and emptied,
the rhythm of life so easily taken for granted.
Now, after a year of sheltering-in-place,
I stand in my living room and assume that same pose.
Breathing deeply, I pray for the army of peaceful warriors
battling an enemy bent on destroying breath itself.

Proxy

The social worker who specializes in grief,
kindly highlights with a yellow marker
all the boxes I need to initial in order to make it legal—
boxes followed by sentences that I don't bother to read
because I know what I am being asked to do
and the disclaimers and stipulations
won't change a thing.

So I sign.
I agree to make decisions for you
when you can no longer make them for yourself.
I will watch the finale from the best seat in the house
and be the one who decides when to stand for the ovation.
We both know where this is going, you said.
And I know how you want to get there.

How many times have we talked about this moment?
While we sat outside the ICU waiting for your mother to die.
While we visited my mother in the hospice called Center for Hope.
While we listened to the machine that breathed for my sister.
Vigils have become commonplace.
Each a rehearsal.
And now we are faced with closing night.
One single light on the stage.
A light you trust me to extinguish.

And so, I do what best friends do.
I make the calls,
hold the phone to your ear.
Witness.
And wait.

I wait until the weight of the decision
is lighter than the weight of your suffering.
Wait until it is no longer a decision
but a completion.
Wait until the waiting is over.

The Nurse Who Brushed Your Hair

We never know which detail
will singe itself into memory.
Perhaps the sound of the machines
all humming different notes.
Perhaps the halting breath,
the false stops and starts,
the fluttering under the eyelids
where some dream still lingers,
or the sheet you kicked off
over and over again
while I pointlessly rearranged it
to protect your privacy.

Perhaps the sound of a phone ringing
in the night is all it will take
to launch me back to that cubicle
where you lay after your last labored breath,
the wild hair that spilled across your pillow
only moments before,
now brushed back from your forehead
into a neat coil at the back of your neck,
your face serene as a pond in August,
and the nurse whose name I never knew
wiping her eyes as she called us in
to say goodbye.

Call Button

She is matter-of-fact
as she carries the bed pan
to the toilet, empties it,
peels off the latex gloves,
fixes my sheet.
Please don't apologize, she says.

Young enough to be my daughter.
Attentive to details I can't begin to discern.
Solving problems I don't even know I have.
And then on to her other seven patients—
to their bedpans and IVs,
stained sheets and unasked questions.
Some cogent enough to say thank you,
others already retreating into silence.

The woman two doors down
howls long into the night,
Help me.
And so she does.
Again and again,
until the woman wears herself out
and falls asleep.

At 3:00 a.m. the nurse wakes me again
to check my vitals.
So sorry to bother you, she says,
Please don't apologize, I reply.

She records my numbers,
pats my arm and says good night.
Two doors down,
the woman moans again.
Help me.
The nurse hears the call and goes,
her footsteps rhythmic
as a beating heart.

Intensive Care

She was eighteen
when she stood at your bedside
in the ICU twenty years ago,
fearlessly stroking your arm,
her eyes moving back and forth
between your face
and the indecipherable monitors
that pinged and buzzed
like the soundtrack to a movie
none of us wanted to see.

As weeks passed,
I watched and witnessed
both an end
and a beginning.

You would be so proud of her now,
proud of the hands that stroke
the arms of patients whose voices
she has never heard.
Proud of how she deciphers
every message and measure
of the monitors whose language
she speaks so fluently.
Proud of the way she explains
with competence and compassion
every detail a sister or niece
or mother needs to know
as they sit at the bedside listening
to the soundtrack of a movie
they never wanted to see.

Love Letter to a Stranger

Yes, it's been a while.
Eighteen years to be exact.
Eighteen years since you sat
across and four seats down from me
on the #6 train from 77th Street to Astor Place,
only one other person in the car
and he sound asleep
in the handicapped seat
that he appeared not to need,
unless you count the desire
to be left alone as a disability.

So in a sense, it was just the two of us.
You watching.
Me weeping.
Did you notice that 77th Street
is the stop at Lenox Hill Hospital?
Did you wonder if I had just received
some dire diagnosis?
Did you see in me some reflection of yourself,
perhaps recalling a scary spot on a mammogram
that left you wondering and afraid?

What was it that led you to exit the train
at the door closest to my seat—
even though there was a closer one
at your end of the car?
Why did you rise a few seconds
before the train pulled into the station,
just so you could pause by my seat and say,
Whatever it is, it will be all right.
It wasn't.
My sister died that day,
and those tears are always
on the brink of falling again.

But I am still here as you predicted.
And now, eighteen years later,
I just want to say I love you,
for taking that moment
when you could have looked away,
but didn't.

E. R. Takayama, Japan

I am an infant once again with fists
balled up in frustration because
I have no words to express my needs.
No tools to take care of myself.

Here in this distant country
where I am a stranger,
where the language is
as alien as I am,

the doctor looks at me
with puzzled eyes
and even my racking cough
sounds foreign to his ears.

My voice croaks from laryngitis,
but that is not why I cannot speak.
I   am   my   words
and my words mean nothing here.

And then the patient woman who,
until now, has simply been
my tour guide, becomes my voice,
explains my situation, guides me
on a different journey from the one
described in the glossy catalogue.

I listen to the rapid utterances
flying back and forth between her
and the doctor who looks at me
while listening to her.

They swim on the rising waves
of a language I will never understand,
and I do the only thing I can do.
I trust them.

Mud Season

It is that other advent,
waiting for that other savior
in the space between the seasons.

It is the squelching sound
of sneakers smeared and sucked
in slippery muck—

The season that hovers
just beyond the flower bed
where the tulips are beginning to tingle—

It is that season that cannot decide
between snow and rain
between lion and lamb—

The comma between
those two bickering siblings
Winter and Spring—

The protracted countdown
to the fulfillment
of a long-awaited promise.

At the Blind Poet's Reading, I Contemplate Deafness

I tell myself it's the acoustics.
The auditorium is vast and the single microphone
no match for the twenty-foot ceiling.
But the shrill siren of tinnitus
conspires with what the doctor called
measurable hearing loss.
The poet's words are muffled
like footfalls in new snow
leaving me alone with my thoughts.

The poet's service dog reclines on the stage
a few feet from the podium.
She sleeps for much of the reading.
She's heard the poems before.
My attention drifts to her twitching
feet as she runs through a dreamscape.
I find myself wishing she would bark—
just a few deep contralto woofs
to tell me that some things will still
ring out clearly like a bell on a buoy
or geese in an October sky.

As the poet talks of Milton,
I think of Beethoven.
I wonder what it might feel like to stand
on the beach in Maine and feel waves
I cannot hear lapping at my feet.
I think of the times I have begged
my rambunctious nephews
to be quiet for just a little while,
and dread the time when I will
have to beg them to speak up.

The poet finishes his reading
and the audience erupts in well earned
and blessedly loud applause.
The dog awakens instantly,
all senses engaged as she returns
to the poet's side. I strain to hear
the tapping of her nails
against the wooden floor
as she escorts her master down the stairs.

Panel Discussion: Writing Poetry in the Aftermath of Suicide

We sit at discrete distances.
No eye contact. No introductions.
Thirty strangers in a room that seats 200.
A fragmented fraternity of grief.

As the speaker's voice fills the cavernous room,
a woman rushes in a few minutes late.
She takes a seat directly behind me.
Her breathing is ragged.
She has run from another session
to hear these poets bear their sorrow.

One after another, they tell
their stories of loss—a mother who washed
down a bottle of pills with a fifth of Scotch.,
a brother who jumped from
the Golden Gate Bridge in the rain,
a sister who simply *took her life.*

In the quiet moments between readings,
I hear her behind me. First sniffles,
then the heavy gulps of swallowed sobs,
then the undisguised weeping
she no longer tries to mask.

Her tears are for a lost one of her own.
Her tears are for each poet at the front of the room.
Her tears are for everyone who has a reason to be here.

When the poets take questions,
someone says, *I can't write about it because
I can't stop crying.* And the poet replies,
Then don't stop crying.
Never stop crying.

I turn to punctuate the poet's advice
with the briefest of smiles.
The first glimpse of my weeping neighbor
reveals a tattooed girl half my age,
in blue hat and torn jeans,
a girl with whom I have nothing
and everything in common.
She responds with a nod.

The shards of her heart are
riddled with unwritten poems,
and as the audience rises to leave,
I want to change just one line
of the hundreds that haunt her.

I wish you peace, I whisper
as we pass each other on the way
to the door. I hear the catch of her breath.
She nods. No introductions.
No explanations. Just one line that I pray
will find a place on her page.

Puzzlement

Our standing phone call.
Every Tuesday night at 8:00 p.m. without fail.
I let the phone ring four times and then hear,
I'm not home right now ... You know what to do.
So I hang up and go back to work on the
crossword puzzle. 44-Down has me stumped.

23-Across, Thomas Edison's middle name.
No brainer. 40-Down, Capitol of Peru.
Come on, that's too easy.
But still no movement on 44-Down.

A half hour later, I call again.
You know what to do ... So this time,
I leave a message. *Hey lady, it's a school night.*
Where the hell are you? And by the way,
what's a 14-letter word for a European cathedral?

At 10:30, I make a cup of herbal tea
and turn my attention back to 44-Down.
Fourth letter 'r'. Notre Dame?
No. Only nine letters.
What's the one in Barcelona?
Why haven't you called back?

The tea is steaming under the lamplight.
Warm vapors whirl above the rim
radiating the scent of peppermint.
It's only when I lift the mug that I notice
my hands are shaking.

I turn on the TV and catch the last half
of *Dirty Dancing* for maybe the hundredth time.
They keep putting Baby in the corner, but
I don't really care because it's after midnight
and you haven't returned my calls.

Sagrada Familia. Fourteen letters.
That's the one. At 2:00 a.m. the phone rings.
A stranger asks, *To whom am I speaking?*
As I tell her my name I know, as sure as I know
Lima is the capitol of Peru, that you are gone.

Visitation

There you are again,
sitting in the blue chair at the foot of my bed.
No words.
Just there.
Always there.

You don't even startle me anymore.
Your visits have become
quite routine,
though I never know
what you'll be wearing.

Sometimes it's the red silk dress
you wore on your thirtieth birthday
when we each spent a week's pay
on dinner at Lutece
and celebrated with Kir Royales.

Sometimes the tweed blazer
you wore in Ireland
where we listened to the ocean
pummeling the rocks eight hundred feet
below the Cliffs of Moher.

Sometimes it's the hospital gown
you wore in the ICU,
while Micah sang Sondheim late into the night
and the nurses stopped what they were doing
just for a moment to hear a familiar refrain.

Now, when I wake
from ever more frequent dreams
in which you appear,
I have stopped asking
why you never speak,

Why you only watch from an armchair
in a corner of my mind.
No words.
Just there.
Always there.

April Snow

An April snowstorm takes us all by surprise—
especially the orange and yellow flame tulips
that bloomed majestically last week
announcing the arrival of spring.

Bowed beneath their burden of snow,
they bend forward in perfect symmetry,
heads nearly touching the ground
like pilgrims praying before a shrine.

By afternoon, the snow has melted.
Standing tall again,
they lift their leaves in alleluias,
bearing witness to resurrection.

Because She Said

—in response to Louise Glück's "Snowdrops"

Because she said,
Winter should have meaning for you,
I paused by the window
and watched the descent
of one snowflake
plucked from the myriad
that drifted past the glass pane.

And because she said,
Yes, risk joy,
I imagined the jubilant journey
of that single flake
from some inestimable height
as it surrendered to the wind
in a trust-fall that carried it
to this exact spot
outside my window.

Then, because she said,
I didn't expect to waken again,
I knew I could close my eyes
and drift to the soft bed that waits for me,
knowing that I too can surrender to
the raw wind of the new world,
like the snowdrops
that wake in spring.

It Figures

My favorite figure
skaters are not
the ones who score
a perfect ten.
My favorites are
the ones who fall.

More specifically,
the ones who fall
and get back up.
without even brushing
the powdered ice
from their bruised behinds.
They just clamber
to their feet and go.

They are my heroes.
Why are there no
gold medals for them?
What is three minutes
of perfection compared to
a lifetime of resilience?

Rise

There is a me-shaped depression
in the left corner of the couch
that tells me I have grown
too accustomed to stillness—
Not the sacred stillness
of the monk in meditation
or the pilgrim at prayer,
but the stillness of stagnation
like water that grows green
with algae when it ceases to flow
or wind chimes that lose their voice
in the absence of a breeze.

> *I watched Mary Poppins*
> *with my great-nephew once.*
> *He could barely contain himself*
> *as he sat on my lap and bounced to the music.*
> *While the credits rolled, he leaped from*
> *the couch and said, Come on, let's dance.*
> *I don't know how, I replied.*
> *And with the wisdom only four-year old*
> *can possess, he said, Well, you'll*
> *never learn to dance sitting on a couch.*

I flip the cushion and plump the throw pillows,
open the blinds and turn off the TV.
One by one, I collect the empty cups
that have accumulated on the coffee table,
stack the magazines that litter the floor.
The months have passed into seasons
and I have grown too comfortable
with isolation, with routines that stiffen
into ruts. A sudden breeze startles
the wind chimes back to life. The sound
is random but musical nonetheless. It calls
to me like church bells. Like my great-nephew
grasping my hand and declaring, *Get up,*
I'll teach you how to dance.

Seven Promises for Daniel

So long awaited,
so suddenly here,
gripping my finger with the mighty
strength of one just 24 hours old.
I am your godmother, dear one.
Not the fairy godmother
who turns pumpkins into coaches
and mice into footmen.
I am neither fairy nor god.
I can't grant wishes,
or make miracles.

I can only make promises,
the sacred silent kind
you won't even know
I am keeping.

I promise to be yes
in a world that will often say no,
to be light in a world
where darkness will fall but
always give way to morning,
to be the lullaby
your memory hears even
when the world
is too loud.

I promise to be the prayer
that never ceases—
the constant presence
that isn't measured by
space or time,
the playmate who
never lets you win at Scrabble,
but keeps playing until you learn
to win on your own.

I promise to be there,
wherever there is,
until the day I die
and every day after that.
And all you need do in return
is simply be.

Nice Boys

I am puzzled when the cruiser pulls up
in front of my nice house
in my nice neighborhood
where my nice grandsons
are climbing the maple tree on our nice lawn.

The officer steps out of the vehicle
and approaches the boys.
Did a neighbor complain?
Are they making too much noise?
By the time I reach the car,
the boys are listening to the officer
who just wants them to know the police are our friends.
She wants them to know they have nothing to fear.
She wants them to know she is nice.

She invites the boys to explore the police car.
Press this button. The lights swirl into action.
Now this one. The siren shrieks to life.
She reaches into the glove compartment,
and hands each a sticker with a silver shield
deputizing them as Junior Officers.
Such nice boys, she says, patting their heads.

Three miles away,
in another part of town,
an officer approaches two little boys.
Their grandmother races down the front steps shaking
as the boys instinctively raise their arms in the air.
Did a stranger make a complaint?
Does their cellphone look too much like a gun?
She fends off memories of sirens and flashing lights.
There's nothing to be afraid of, officer, she gasps.
These are nice boys.

I Just Have to Say

Or maybe I don't.
Maybe I just have to listen.

Maybe I can take a breath, take a walk
take the time to ask, *What can I do for you?*

Maybe being right isn't as important
as being kind.

Maybe the world will keep turning
even if I don't air my list of grievances.

Maybe the sun will shine, and the birds will sing,
and the flowers will bloom without benefit of my bluster.

Maybe the unsaid word is more eloquent
than the unnecessary declaration.

Maybe not always, but maybe right now,
I can make a quiet space for peace.

Eating My Words

If my words were food arranged
on the shelves of my refrigerator,
which ones would I choose to consume?

Would I mindlessly grab
the nearest empty calories?
Or reach behind the leftovers
to the fresh blueberries
I bought at the farmer's market?

I know how to feed my body.
I would carefully rinse
the berries in cold water
and stir them into a bowl
of rich creamy yogurt
with just a few sprinkles
of granola for texture.

Why don't I choose my words
with the same care, taking in only
the ones that provide sustenance?
Why do I gorge on words

that are sour, rancid, undigestible,
stuffing myself with criticism,
choking on expletives I would
never serve a guest at my table.

I want to purge these cold shelves,
dispose of all that does not nourish,
pour the sour words down the drain
like milk gone bad.

Thank You Will Smith

Thank you for striding up to the stage
accompanied by Ali, and King Richard,
and the Fresh Prince, and all their brethren
and in one out-of-control controlled moment
bringing your open hand down
on the cheek of the open-mouthed.

Thank you for two days of distraction
when the biggest story on earth
was a slap—so much easier to condemn
or condone than say, I don't know, a war maybe.

Thank you for the space you took up
on the front page of *The New York Times*
that pre-empted a few inches of tragedy
and for the follow-up stories in *The Washington Post*
and CNN. Heck, even Fox News took a time-out
from sowing hysteria to gape at the spectacle.

Thank you for that moment when you
ignited more moral indignation than, say,
world hunger, or melting ice caps, or body counts.
So good to come up for air,
to hear the thump of a palm across a cheek
instead of a bomb blowing a city to rubble.

Were you Galahad standing up for the maiden fair,
or the schoolyard bully beating up the class clown?
Who knows . . . who cares?
For one moment even the bombs
shattering Mariupol must have
held their breath and waited
to see if it was scripted
or the real thing.

Another Prayer to St. Anthony

St. Anthony, St. Anthony, please come around...

How many times have you helped me find
my car keys,
my glasses,
my other shoe.

Something is lost and can't be found...

There was even that time
Max got out of the yard
and we thought he was gone for good
as we searched everywhere,
calling his name and listening for his bark
until at last, I got back to the house,
clutching your name like a rosary,
and found him waiting for me by the door.

St. Anthony, St. Anthony, please come around...

There have been times when,
rebuking myself for carelessness,
I have refrained from calling on you,
telling myself it was my own fault,
and you had bigger fish to fry,
until I finally gave up and called your name,
and reached into a forgotten pocket
only to find, yet again, those keys
that seem to have a mind of their own.

Something is lost and can't be found...

St. Anthony, I have searched every dusty corner,
every closet shelf,
under every bed,
to no avail.
And so I turn to you again,

to help me find what I have lost . . .
My country, St. Anthony,
My faith in justice,
My hope.

Algorithm and Blues

I am a demographic data point
with a good credit rating and a Visa card,
a white, female, middle aged, over-weight,
animal-lover who reliably clicks on videos
of three-legged dogs, wounded pelicans, and/or
deer trapped on thin ice rescued by brave
outdoorsy men in Carhartt overalls
who risk all to rescue Bambi's
great-great-grand-deer from doom.

I am a tree-hugging, bird-watching,
liberal Democrat likely to sign
petitions for environmental reform,
reuse plastic bags and bubble wrap,
and save scrap paper for future use
thereby placing me in the target market
for dry detergent sheets and compost bins
and recycled anything.

I am a mathematical construct
comprised of sequential codes,
corollaries and outcomes.
As such, Amazon knows
what I will do long before I do it.
But just what will that be
when all the Fulfillment Centers
are empty, and the rain forests
are reduced to ashes?

What to Say When

It's the unwanted skill
we hone over time
only after we have uttered
the tone-deaf encouraging word
that is somehow received graciously
by the one who grieves
like one more stone
in a backpack full of rocks.

We lay down the burden
of our helplessness as if it were a gift
and expect it to be carried
by the one we wish to comfort—
well-intentioned words that bear the weight
of our own impotence.

It is only after we have sat
at the bedside of the dying,
or stood at the front of the receiving line
as mourners grasp for the right word,
that we come to understand
the blessing of silent presence.

We learn it from the friend
who has the courage to say nothing,
the grace to sit quietly and offer support
like the steel beam that holds up
some small portion of a crumbling bridge
without ever saying a word.

News for the Real World

This morning, I want to wake up with no headlines.
I want to find that my *New York Times*

has been replaced with a worn-out copy
of *The Velveteen Rabbit*,

and the Skin Horse is inviting me
to love the world in all its broken realness.

I want to touch the Earth where the soft fur
has been rubbed off and see it with my fingertips.

When I feel the need to know who is fighting with whom,
and what disaster occurred overnight, I want to hear

that soft tattered rabbit whisper in the breeze,
I am as real as anything you will find on the front page.

When the hard facts are just too hard, I want to press
the worn velveteen ears to my cheek and remember

that the hot cup of tea, and the warm blanket,
and the beloved sleeping beside me

are every bit as real as the rage that fuels the news,
and for today I want to embrace the real I can touch

with my hands and see with my eyes,
and let the world rage on without me.

Murmuration

The first time I saw one,
I had to pull off the road,

too wound up in wonder to wonder why.
I simply gazed at the aerial choreography:

Murmuration, a wave of starlings
whirling and wheeling across the sky.

Meditation in motion,
Lava lamp lit in the winter dusk.

Fibonacci sequence of spirals spinning
into funnel clouds and coiling flows—

shapeshifting curtain in constant motion—
black rose blooming across the horizon—

mammoth butterfly with undulating wings —
beating heart aloft in the fading light.

A thousand wings murmur on the wind.
I merely murmur, Amen.

Now That I Know

Now is the time to know
That all you do is sacred.
　　　　　—Hafiz

I will live today as if I know
that all I do is sacred.

I will shower under clean water that purifies all
it touches, including this body that I too often neglect.

I will pour my coffee and yours as if each mug
were a chalice brimming with a holy offering.

I will make our bed with cool white sheets
like clean Irish linens spread across an altar.

I will fold our clothes like origami cranes
and arrange them like ceremonial vestments.

Hafiz says he is a divine envoy upon whom
the Beloved has written a holy message.

I unfold that message like an ancient scroll
and find the only truth I need to know:

If I do everything with love
each chore is a sacrament.

Sometimes the Muse

is an 87-year-old man with Alzheimer's
who clutches the greased rope of memory
long enough to call and say,
Remember that thing you said about God?
And trust?
That was good.
Write a poem about that.

A poet himself, he doesn't remember
that he once wrote about the sequence
of flowers blooming seventeen miles a day
as Spring travels from South to North.

But he remembers that you asked him
if he still prays. He remembers that
you asked him to channel his trust in God
into trusting the loved ones
who remind him daily that who he was
remains who he is,
even if he forgets their names.

A preacher long ago,
he remembers congregations
who trusted him and how he earned that trust,
and how he loved their reliance upon him,
even as he resists relying on others now.

Remember that thing you said
about sadness, and about my wife
crying about the disease,
and not because I have let her down?
That was good.
Write a poem about that.

Reflexology Lesson

Take a firm hold of the foot.
Slowly apply pressure.
Listen to the foot's response.
When it twitches or jerks
it is telling a story.

Though your hands
will never leave the feet,
you will touch every part of the body,
every crevice and appendage,
every nerve and muscle.
You must think of it
as a sacred act.

Don't worry about incense
or candles or music.
Let the rhythm of the breath
fill the room.
It is music enough.

When the client thanks you,
and says she has never felt better,
don't let it go to your head.
You can cure nothing.
You only provide a quiet space
for the body to heal itself—
if only for a little while.

Take meticulous notes.
there will come a time
when it will be important to know
that your right thumb
pressing the reflexes along the
anterior ridge of the left foot,

helped bring thirty minutes
of peaceful sleep to the client
who was tormented by insomnia
in the months before she leaped
from the eleventh-story window.

What the Map Makers Knew

Beyond this place,
there be dragons.

She dwells in the place
the old map makers could not chart—
the place without names,
where waters churn and the open mouths
of empty caves gape along the shoreline.

All those years telling her children,
There are no monsters here.
The ritual of opening and
closing closet doors,
getting down on her knees
to prove there were only
dust bunnies under the bed.

Now she lies under the covers
in a room she did not choose,
a photo on the night stand
of someone she once knew by name.
Her children are scattered east and west.
They call every Sunday
without fail. I tell them she is well,
refer to her chart. Relay facts.

A wildlife calendar hangs
on the wall at the foot of her bed,
a long-ago Christmas gift
from her daughter in Pittsburgh.
A lion presides over a slab of stone
somewhere on the African savannah,
scanning the horizon,
keeping beasts at bay.
She wakes each morning
under his protective gaze.

I tried to turn the page once,
but she wept like a baby
ripped from a dream.
So I left it as I found it
in that room where it is
forever February.

The Harlot's Version

I saw their faces.
The righteous keepers of holy law.
I wouldn't look away,
even as they spat in my hair
and gripped my arms,
purpling my flesh with their thumb prints
while they dragged me to the Mount of Olives,
calling me adulteress and whore.

They took me to the rabbi,
The one called Jesus.
I heard him preach in the town square one time.
Love your neighbor, he said.
Which of my neighbors
watched my comings and goings?
Decided my body was a vessel of sin
deserving death at the hands of a mob
pelting me with a torrent of rocks?

Yes, I sinned. I never said I didn't.
But no one ever asked me why.
And I didn't sin alone.
Where was my partner in crime
while they scooped up stones
by the handful to fling at my head?

They dangled me in front of the rabbi
like bait on a hook,
waiting to see if he would follow their law
or smash it to pieces
the way they wanted to smash me.
*Let him who is without sin among you
be the first to throw a stone at her.*

When you read about it someday,
you will no doubt be impressed
by his calm dismantling of the mob.
But as I lifted my head to thank him,
I watched the crowd disperse
and even as they skulked down the mountain path,
I saw them stooping to slip a few extra stones
in their pockets—
always at the ready for another day.

Instructions for the Morning after the Terrible Haircut

First, do not look in the mirror
until after you have had your coffee.
Everything looks better after coffee.
When it still does not look better,
do not drink a second cup of coffee.
It will not make your hair grow faster,
and it will make you jittery while wondering
if anyone would find it odd
if you showed up at work
wearing a bee-keeper's bonnet.

Next, go to your jewelry box and take out
the largest pair of earrings you own—
the ones with peacock feathers and beads,
to draw attention away from the terrible haircut.
Then dig out the tube of red lipstick
you bought last New Year's Eve and swore
you would never wear again
because it made you look like a clown.
Nothing distracts from a terrible haircut
like a crimson neon sign across your face

Before heading out the door,
sit still for a little while
and listen to the morning news.
No, I mean really listen.
Then go back and wash your face.
Return to your usual
understated silver earrings.
Be thankful that this morning,
a terrible haircut
is your biggest problem.

An Invisible Form of Sadness

*—a cento in homage to Galway Kinnell,
using 31 lines from 31 of his poems*

I love to go out in late September.
The whole compass is visible.
I want to turn and look back.
I leave my eyes open.
An electric force grabs my feet.

You might not still be blossoming when I go back.
The hollyhock falls before finishing its blossoming.
After the beginning and before the end, it is green.
Everything flowers from within of self-blessing.
And for one moment we know we exist.

We stand on the shore which is mist beneath us.
In the stillness again the shore lights remember.
Looking back, I have to squint to see those days.
For us, back then, to live seemed almost to die.
The door closes on pain and confusion.

In the half darkness, we look at each other.
I remember those summer nights.
Clouds come over the moon
when the moon lies full on the sea.
Its deeper darkness might absorb me.

How am I ever going to be able to say this?
The flowers turn to husks.
The promise was too freely broken.
Another life is upon us.
That is how we have learned, the embrace is all.

Living brings you to death, there is no other road.
Often we forget, and imagine we are immortal.
On the brink of our happiness, we stop.
Ours was a wonderful party.
Goodbye, dear friend.

❧

All selections from *Collected Poems of Galway Kinnell*, 2017.

Title. "Pure Balance"
 1. "Blackberry Eating"
 2. "Tillamook Journal"
 3. "Lava"
 4. "Middle of the Way"
 5. "The Cat"
 6. "Flower of Five Blossoms"
 7. "Testament of the Thief"
 8. "Freedom, New Hampshire"
 9. "St. Francis and the Sow"
 10. "Gravity"
 11. "The River that is East"
 12. "First Day of the Future"
 13. "The Striped Snake and the Goldfinch"
 14. "Astonishment"
 15. "The Room"
 16. "After Making Love, We Hear Footsteps"
 17. "The Still Time"
 18. "On the Tennis Court at Night"
 19. "Told by Seafarers"
 20. "Turkeys"
 21. "Last Holy Fragrance"
 22. "Cells Breathe in the Emptiness"
 23. "The Avenue Bearing the Initial of Christ into the New World"
 24. "The Old Life"
 25. "Goodbye"
 26. "Lastness"
 27. "Holy Shit"
 28. "Flower Herding on Mount Monadnock"
 29. "For the Lost Generation"
 30. "Farewell"

Four Seasons

Fly in pirouettes
above the ice-scrimmed branches
of the sycamores that lift their arms
to tango with the winter moon.

Bloom like the first tulip
that drinks the April sun
as if it were a river of light
pouring into its open throat.

Hike the canyon floor
immersed in an ocean of silence
interrupted only by the flutter
of a butterfly's wings
as she flits past your left ear.

Run ice cold water
over the ripe red apples
you picked this morning
from the tree in your backyard
paradise sweet and tart
and unadorned.

Let no season leave you untouched
by the throbbing air
that signs its name in red on your cheeks,
be it the chill wind of winter
or the August sunburn
that peels away the layers
to the tender flesh beneath.

Vermont Summer Rain

Because I know you can't love
The Green Mountain State
without loving the thing that makes it green,
I resign myself to a morning walk
in the rain that has persisted since dawn.
I snap the leash onto my dog's collar
and explain to her that yes,
even though it is cold and wet,
it is time for us to venture out.

Her short legs resist
the gentle tug of the leash
as I try to coax her to the door.
She understands wet.
She understands cold.
But she doesn't understand
the precious gift of rain.

So I pick her up,
carry her to the edge of the woods
where I relish the smell of wet grass
and generous perfume of pine trees
and despite my sodden feet,
I can't help but love
this symbiosis of water and earth,
even as it soaks my hair
and dampens every stitch of clothing.

Rosie squats and shivers
and shakes off the raindrops
that sequin her fur,
oblivious to the miracle
in which we are immersed.

And as I bow down to pet her head
and tell her she's a good girl,
the tapping of the raindrops
on the leaves sounds like
a thousand mittened hands clapping,
telling us we are both good girls,
we are both part of this greening,
this baptism in the woods,
this verdant summer sacrament.

Prayer for a Miracle in the Newsroom

I pray for the ghost of Walt Whitman to take over the editor's desk,
filling the daily papers with good news . . . and news of the good

News of the bus driver who waits at the corner on a rainy day
News of the baker who donates his bread to the soup kitchen

News of the nurse who washes vomit from the patient's face
News of the teenager who shovels his neighbor's walk

News of the neighbor who looks in on the lady in 3E
when she hasn't seen her in a few days

News of the postal worker who sends a get well card
to the old man who receives nothing but medical bills

News that in its quiet dailiness merits no headlines
News that defies our notion of what's fit to print

Fault Lines

We sift
through
the rubble
like desperate
seismologists
after an
earthquake.

We seek
only
the fault
line,
wanting it
to be straight,
pointing
to an answer,
a reason,
a target.

The shifting
plates are
jagged—
cracks
radiate
in every
direction.

Obsessed
with fault,
we ignore the
aftershocks
that threaten
to swallow us
whole.

Mr. Gutenberg Respectfully Declines
Mr. Zuckerberg's Friend Request

Dear Mr. Zuckerberg:
Thank you for your Friend Request.
I must respectfully decline
due to the unfortunate circumstance
that I am dead—
which limits my social network greatly.

In the interest of updating my Timeline,
it appears, good sir, that I died of poisoning
from my own invention.
The alloy of lead, tin and antimony took its toll.
So sad when one's own creation
plants the seeds of his demise.

You have said, *Move fast and break things.*
Unless you are breaking stuff,
you are not moving fast enough.
I too felt the urge to break things—
to break the silence,
to break the barriers to truth.
It was I, after all, who said,

> *Let us break the seal*
> *which seals up holy things,*
> *and give wings to Truth*
> *in order that she may win every soul*
> *that comes into the world by her word*
> *no longer written at great expense*
> *by hands easily palsied,*
> *but multiplied like the wind*
> *by an untiring machine.*

That very wind can scatter seeds
to take root and grow,
or whirl out of control.
But I am sure, Friend,
that you are aware of such risks.
And so, I leave you, good sir,
with my most sincere good wishes—
to Like or not, as you see fit.

Your most humble Friend,
Johannes Gutenberg

Epithalamion for Margie and Ed

Four white orchids on her blue lapel.
His one grey suit fresh from the cleaners.
Practical and neat from day one,
my parents smile out from the only portrait
that survives them.

She was nineteen, he twenty-nine,
a World War separated the girl who waved
goodbye as he left in uniform,
and the woman he discovered upon his return.
She saw Tyrone Powers in his blue Irish eyes.
He saw little Margie all grown up.

The city was smaller then.
They commuted to separate jobs—
He, operating the mayonnaise mixer at Kraft Foods,
She, working the conveyor belt at a paper bag factory,
until the baby came along.

Into that child they poured
all the joy they had never known
as children. In each other,
they found peace enough to share.

If time is the measure of a marriage,
theirs was short. Her heart broke
when his stopped beating.
But whenever she saw white orchids,
she told the story of the day they stood
before the judge at City Hall and said
'til death do us part.

Now both gone,
and that first child too,
but oh, how the white orchids bloom
in the pot on my windowsill,
a daily declaration of promises kept.

Legacy

From my mother,
I inherited silence—
the cave where anger goes to die,
or at least to get buried.
A sailor's silence, I thought,
when she hissed,
Shhh, don't rock the boat.
A silence that clutched her throat
hotter than tears,
tighter than a clenched fist.

From my father,
I inherited a broken heart—
A heart that attacks
without warning
like a mountain lion
lunging from a tree,
a heart that constricts in the chest
like a clenched fist,
a heart that shatters the silence
like a siren in the night.

Assembling the Perfect Father

He didn't live long enough
to disappoint me,
so from the time
I was four years old,
I assembled him from
celluloid images of perfection.

My father was as strong as John Wayne,
as handsome as Tyrone Power,
as quiet as Henry Fonda,
as protective as Rin Tin Tin,
as thoughtful as Gregory Peck,
as funny as Bob Hope,
as tender as Jimmy Stewart.

My father was every dream
Hollywood had to offer.
He was the movie star
I would watch again and again
until the final frame announced
The End.

You Just Never Know

My mother never practiced yoga.
She never studied comparative religions
or sought to find herself in the silence
of rustic mountain retreats.

Her mudra was a cigarette poised
between the fingers of her right hand
and a coffee cup cradled in her left.

Her mantra was simple.
With a slow exhalation,
she would bring it forth
from the silence—
You just never know . . .

I invoke her wisdom
when a driver cuts me off in traffic
and I want to feel compassion
instead of rage—
You just never know where he's going
or why he's racing to get there.

I seek her grace
when I feel inclined to roll my eyes
at the woman in the supermarket
holding up the line while she fumbles
with a bundle of coupons—
You just never know if her children
had enough to eat last night.

I think of her when I look at
myself in the mirror
stretching my limbs
in a sun salutation,
her voice urging me
to create space for compassion.

Encounter on Route 169

One summer evening, my mother loaded us
into the car that never passed inspection
and drove along Route 169
to a deserted service road in Bayonne
where acres of oil tanks were surrounded
by tall grass and a chain link fence.

She told my brother and me
to hold out our hands palms up
as she dropped sugar cubes
from a brown paper bag,
then told us to reach
through the fence and wait.

But what are we doing here? I whispered.
Shhh, she replied, pointing a finger
to something moving in the grass.
I followed her eyes and saw two
shaggy horses ambling our way.

They were the first horses I had ever seen
that didn't have cops astride their backs.
She held my wrist to keep my hand steady
while the caramel horse with the blond tail
bent its head and parted it velvety lips
to take the sugar cubes from my small palm.

I squealed the squeal that fuses fear with delight,
wondering how she found this spot in the shadow
of factories and power lines,
where horses and goats and sheep
could be seen and touched and fed.
Wondered how she learned to braid
the threads of an urban childhood
into the mane of an unfettered horse.

Spunk

It's what Rosie the Riveter had
rolled up in the sleeve
of her blue work shirt
as she declared, *We can do it!*

It's what Nancy Drew had
as she darted across town in her
yellow roadster solving crimes
in a stylish trench coat and beret.

Surely it's what Bette Davis had
when she warned her friends to
Fasten your seatbelts,
it's going to be a bumpy night.

It's what my mother had
when she marched up to PS 17
to confront the seventh-grade teacher
who delighted in bullying me.

It's what she relied on when
she told him if he made me cry again,
I wouldn't be the only one
coming home from school in tears.

It's what I have
when I would rather be quiet
and mind my own business
but can't because I am her daughter.

It's Debatable

—for my mother

Let a smile be your umbrella.
> *But then I will get very, very wet.*

Always say please and thank you.
> *But what if someone offers me a haggis sandwich?*

Mind your P's and Q's.
> *But who's going to mind the rest of the alphabet?*

Make your bed every morning.
> *But doesn't that mean I have to get out of it?*

Wear sensible shoes.
> *But they're ugly and they don't match my pajamas*

If you can't say something nice, don't say anything at all.
> *But then I will be literally speechless.*

Sit like a lady.
> *But why do ladies have to sit around all the time?*

Drink eight glasses of water every day.
> *But then I'll have to make eight trips to the bathroom every day.*

Get eight hours of sleep every night.
> *But how can I do that if I'm running back and forth to the bathroom?*

Treat others as you would have them treat you.
> *But . . . but . . . Okay, you win.*

To My Stepson on Mother's Day

A fraught phrase indeed,
bent under the weight
of Cinderella's grasping interloper
and Sleeping Beauty's apple-wielding witch.

Better to say,
my father's wife.
Less literary baggage
and no less accurate.

But you made a different choice.
Nothing dramatic.
No naming ceremony.
Just a simple introduction.

This is my stepmom.
A small thing to some
But not, I think, to you . . .
Nor me.

Although I played no role
in making you the man you are,
you chose, with one word,
to extend the invitation
only I could accept.

Step in, you said.
Step into my life.
Step into my heart.
Step into my family.

Meeting Emily

When your future stepdaughter is an entomologist,
you have to rethink your relationship with bugs.
A bee is not a flying weapon out to puncture tender flesh,
but a highly specialized aviator,
willing to lay down its life for his community.
Ants are not picnic invaders but engineers,
teaching us how to work together for the common good.

Meeting her in Florida for the first time,
I am determined to make a good impression.
A glass of chardonnay and small talk around the patio,
while a palmetto bug shoots back and forth like a comet at my feet.
I will not shriek like the city girl I am and always will be.
I will not flee to the insect-free screened porch.
Show no fear, I tell myself, as I squeeze her father's hand.
But when she sees me cringing at the infernal buzzing,
she scoops the bug up in her hand and gently places it
in the bed of myrtle edging the garden.
She is the epitome of cool and warmth.

Ten years later, I still hate bugs.
But oh, how I love Emily.

Papa Will Help

Lower lip trembling,
the two-year-old wails,
hands balled up into tiny fists,
burbling a tearful lament
as the adults try fruitlessly
to decipher his urgent
but incoherent message.

After a few minutes
of listening to the
breathless sobs,
his father says,
Use your words, son.
Papa will help,
Just use your words—

Haltingly,
words emerge.
        Hungry...
        Sleepy...
        Afraid...

Perhaps this
is where poetry
begins.

And prayer.

Clean Up in Aisle Three

The loudspeaker announces
a shattered jar of spaghetti sauce
and within minutes
an aproned man appears with a mop.
Soon the marinara is reduced
to no more than a fading aroma
and the broken glass is swept up
and deposited safely into a trash can.

Meanwhile in Aisle Four
famine and disease
are littering the unwashed floor.
All the shelves in Aisle Five
are collapsing under
the weight of injustice
and Aisle Six . . . well,
don't even ask about Aisle Six.

And where is that guy with the mop?
Who is going to clean up this mess?
The store is getting ready to close
and there's disaster everywhere you look.
And where, oh where,
do I find the milk and eggs?

The Earth Moved

No really, it moved.
It moved in a straight line
from the backyard fence
to where I sat in the grass,
where I never sit,
which is probably why
I have never seen it before.

Never seen the evidence
of a tiny creature drilling
through the muck,
with pink paws like paddles
tunneling 'round rocks and roots
on a subterranean superhighway
of his own invention.

So this is one of those molehills
I have always turned into mountains—
the handiwork of a velvety creature
not much larger than a mouse,
whose aptitude for finding its way
through the dark,
might just be a lesson for us all.

What a person wants

is a dog. Really. What a person wants
is the warm press of fur and muscle
that coils itself into the small of your back
and nearly pushes you off the bed
in the middle of the night,

the swish of the tail that sweeps everything off the coffee table,
including the crystal wine glass you just filled with cabernet
that spreads like a purple bruise across your white carpet.

What you really want is the smelly residue that lingers
on your hand after the dog has licked it uncontrollably
for the sheer joy of your return from the grocery store.

What we all want is that thing that makes us willing
to have our hearts not just broken, but shattered
like a windshield hit by a stone at 65 mph,
when the vet says, *I think it's time now.*

Quiet Waves

A quiet wave breaks over me
every time I open the door
where our dog no longer waits
for the turn of the knob.

It swells again at dinner time when
a piece of chicken falls to the floor
       and stays there
until I bend to pick it up,

When the lint filter comes out clean
and I wonder if the dryer has malfunctioned
until I realize what it hasn't captured,
and why,

When I pull last winter's black sweater from the drawer
and find short white hairs clinging to the fiber—
once a nuisance, now a *memento mori*
I pluck from the wool strand by strand.

Adirondack Morning Meditation

Eight women tread a late summer trail.
Pine needles and moss muffle our steps.

We have made a pact.
No talking for this one sacred hour.

In the distance the burble of a stream
penetrates the thick-barked bank of trees.

A woodpecker taps out his own Morse Code
while a red squirrel translates from a birch branch.

We tap each other's shoulders pointing mutely at
a bouquet of red-tinged mushrooms blooming

in a twist of pine roots like a fist full of peonies,
poisonous probably, but lovely in the morning light.

At a bend in the trail, we linger on a footbridge
listening to dragonflies darting past our ears.

How hard it is to swallow the sound of awe
as it rises in our throats.

That Day

I think of all the ways
it could have been different.
I could have been out sick that day.
You could have gotten a flat tire
on the Palisades Parkway.
I could have had back-to-back meetings,
You could have looked at your watch
instead of saying yes to a second cup of coffee.

Instead, you arrived at my office
on a sunny summer day with plenty of time
to check off each agenda item
while unspooling a thread of conversation
that felt like it had begun a lifetime ago.

Instead, I walked you to your car
and had to fight the impulse to kiss you
because, after all, such things are simply not done
at the end of a business meeting
with someone you just met two hours ago.

Instead, we shook hands
and exchanged business cards,
and looked forward to working together
in the months ahead,

each moment conspiring with the next
to bring about what some would call
love at first sight, or destiny,
or even a small series of coincidences
that just happened to happen.

But fifteen years later, I still call it
what I have always known it to be:
a miracle.

Five Things to Never Write a Poem About

The rainbow afghan
my mother crocheted fifty years ago—
a collage of remnant yarns
to wrap me in all the colors
she could squeeze into one blanket.

The wet freckled nose of the dog
we adopted from the shelter
two days before he would have been put down,
who looks at you with eyes that seem to know
you said yes despite your allergies.

The smile on your face
in that first photo of the two of us
together,
taken by a stranger long before
selfies were the all the rage.

That first cup of coffee in the morning
when the aroma fills the kitchen
like burning incense
and the dark brew fills the belly
like glowing embers in a warm hearth.

You, drenched in mud and sweat,
back bent in what you call a good ache
coming in from the garden
to wash the fragrant soil
from under your fingernails.

These simple images.
shameless in their contentedness,
chronicling the most mundane of miracles,
confirm what I have known all along—
I'll never make it as a poet.

But as I carry that steaming cup of coffee to you
stretched out in our bed under my mother's afghan,
resting your back after toiling in the garden
with our goofy dog by your side,
I watch that glorious smile cross your face,

And I can live with that.

Last Poem and Testament

When you finally get around
to packing up the last vestiges
of scraps and mementoes
I once thought important,
don't be surprised
when you find a scribbled note
tucked into the bottom
of my underwear drawer.
Just unfold it to see
what I left behind
in some forgotten
attempt at a poem.
And this is what it will say ...

Thank you—no more, no less.
Thank you for gusts of wind
spewing spindrift into our faces
on the shore at Pemaquid.
Thank you for Mountain Avens
and Ladies Bedstraw
springing up between the stones
of the Burren.
Thank you for climbing
776 steps of the Eiffel Tower
to watch dusk drape itself
over Paris like a shawl.
Thank you for midnight sun
in Iceland and mirco-orchids
in El Junque.

Thank you for home—
for hand-hewn birdhouses
and tulips every spring,
for snow tires on Valentine's Day—
a more practical way to say
I love you.

Thank you for everything
that made this life
just a little harder to let go of,
and thank you most of all
for making heaven
feel downright
redundant.

Tell Me

I don't need a scale
to tell me I'm thin enough.
(I never will be).

I don't need a watch
to tell me I'm on time.
(I never am).

I don't need a mirror
to tell me I'm beautiful.
(I wouldn't believe it).

I don't need you
to tell me you love me—
But when you do,

I know what makes flowers
bloom in the desert
after soft rains.

So tell me again.
and I will tell you
every day—

Even when we think
we don't need
to hear the words.

Meditations in the Subjunctive Mood

What if Fulfillment Centers were not warehouses full of excess,
    but classrooms full of promise?

What if global warming were not an environmental catastrophe,
    but a wave of worldwide friendship?

What if symbols were not more important
    than what they symbolize?

What if peace could not be torn to pieces
    by those who preach ideologies instead of ideals?

What if left and right
    were actually two halves of a whole?

What if we chose dialogue over diatribe,
    involvement over invective,
    civility over civil strife?

Winter Light

Now.
Right now,
while sunlight
penetrates the icicles
fringing the roof-line
like crystal champagne flutes
held aloft for a toast.

Now.
Right now,
while Cardinals
grace the snow-covered
backyard like red roses
arranged on a linen
altar cloth.

Now.
Right now,
while a brilliant
winter sun delights
the hearty souls
who witness
her brief
but brilliant
apparition.

Now.
Write now,
while winter light
illuminates
the blanketed fields
that gleam like a
clean sheet of paper
begging you to begin.

What Is More Generous Than a Window?

—a cento comprised of lines from Poetry of Presence:
An Anthology of Mindfulness Poems

Stop whatever it is you're doing.
Come, let's stand by the window.
I have seen the sun break through.
Together, we are a tribe of eyes that look upward.
The evening arrives; we look up and it is there.
Invisible birds sing to the memory of light.

The trees stand like twenty-seven prophets in a field.
Whatever it is, the trees know
every thought and action is sacred.
Wherever you are is called Here.
What fools we were, not to have seen
from the place we are right now.

The world is still beautiful.
Go and open the door.

❧

Sources:

1. "The Patience of Ordinary Things," Pat Schneider
2. "On How to Pick and Eat Poems," Phyllis Cole-Dai
3. "Thinking," Danusha Lameris
4. "The Bright Field," R.S. Thomas
5. "We are a Tribe," Alberto Rios
6. "Surprised by Evening," Robert Bly
7. "Still Life at Dusk," Rosemerry Wahtola Trommer
8. "I am Going to Start Living Like a Mystic," Edward Hirsch
9. "Learning from Trees," Grace Butcher
10. "Now is the Time," Hafiz (translation by Daniel Ladinsky)
11. "Lost," David Wagoner
12. "Meeting the Light Completely," Jane Hirschfield
13. "The Place Where We are Right," Yehuda Amichai,
    (translation by Chana Bloch and Stephen Mitchell)

14. "Testimony," Rebecca Baggett
15. "the door," Miraslov Holub (translation by Ian and Jarmila Milneret, et al)

Planning the Funeral

—for Nancy Kepler

Easier than planning a wedding.
No seating chart or RSVPs.
And yet, there are arrangements to make.
Guests to consider.
And of course, the dress.

She tells me the plans
over tea in her quiet den.
Would you like another cookie, dear?
After my polite reply,
she returns to the subject at hand.
Pink flowers, she declares.
All pink. Roses, lilies, the whole shebang.

And the 23rd Psalm, of course.
Not because it's customary—
because it's the cornerstone
of her ongoing conversation with God.

She has chosen a favorite poem
to be read from the altar,
a poem she wrote herself for the occasion.
After all, she giggles. *I want to be there, too!*

I am puzzled by the ease
with which she navigates her agenda.
Should I change the subject?
Comfort her with assurances of longevity.
Remind her she is the picture of health
and has nothing to fear?

But she has no fear.
Needs no assurances.
At eighty-seven, she is ready for the journey,
and planning her farewell party.
I just like to leave things tidy, she says.

Gratitude

You ask me to count my blessings.
Easier to ask an ant
to count the petals of a peony.
Circumnavigating her pink planet,
she scales her supple landscape,
each petal revealing
a new surface to explore.
She will always lose count,
so lost in that sweet nectar.

I am that ant,
drunk on the sweetness
that surrounds me,
grateful for every blessing,
but powerless
to count that high.

Autobiography of a Poem

I am the poem that will never grace
the pages of *The New Yorker*.
I will never be read and analyzed
in grad school courses where experts
dissect lines and metaphors like cadavers.

I am a door with no lock offering easy access
and an invitation to stay awhile.
I am the slender volume on the nightstand
of the retired English professor in Texas
who tells me this is where she keeps the books
she likes to read before going to sleep.

I am the wrinkled sheet of paper
folded into eighths
that you keep in your wallet
so that it's close at hand
when you don't want to feel so alone.
I am the poem you sink into
like the over-stuffed chair
in your grandmother's parlor.

I am not famous,
or complicated,
or especially brilliant.
But if I have ever made you think
and feel and revisit me
when you needed company,
I have lived a good life,
and done my job.

Terms and Conditions

—a prose poem in the age of the app

Users are required to read and accept the following terms and conditions.

Upon reading all terms and conditions, click the box at the bottom and proceed to the next window.

Caution: Do not skip to the little box at the bottom and click Agree. That's how we got into this mess in the first place.

1. This site guarantees that your identity will not be stolen. But it might be revealed in ways you may have overlooked while posting comments on Facebook.
2. This site uses cookies. Generally, Oreos. Always best when shared with Friends.
3. This site engages in political subversion. It makes no secret of its intent to infiltrate partisan despair with radical joy.
4. This site does not care where you ate dinner last night or what you had for dessert. It will not upload images of the orgasmic risotto for which you paid $42 at a 5-star restaurant which will still find its way through your bowels tomorrow morning whether you capture it for posterity or not.
5. This site employs human intelligence. No artificial ingredients.
6. This site provides 24-hour customer support. To access it, close your eyes. Find a quiet place. Listen.
7. This site is powered by faith, hope and love. The user accepts all related risks, rewards and responsibilities.

If you agree to all of the terms and conditions listed above, check the box and proceed to the next window.

No. Not the window on your computer screen.

The window that offers the best view of the sky.

Open it ... Breathe.

Begin.

GLORIA HEFFERNAN's *Exploring Poetry of Presence* (Back Porch Productions) won the 2021 CNY Book Award for Nonfiction. She also received the 2022 Naugatuck River Review Narrative Poetry Prize. Heffernan is the author of the collections *Peregrinatio: Poems for Antarctica* (Kelsay Books) and *What the Gratitude List Said to the Bucket List*, (New York Quarterly Books). Her chapbook *Animal Grace* was selected for the Keystone Chapbook Series. Her work has appeared in over one hundred publications, including *Poetry of Presence II* (Grayson Books). Heffernan turned her attention to poetry on a full-time basis after a thirty-year career in higher education administration at numerous institutions, including New York University, Pace University, and Le Moyne College. Her focus was community service, service learning, and community engagement. Currently, she teaches poetry at Syracuse YMCA's Downtown Writers Center. For more information: www. gloriaheffernan.wordpress.com

www.ingramcontent.com/pod-product-compliance
Lightning Source LLC
Chambersburg PA
CBHW072147090426
42739CB00013B/3301